I CAN READ ABOUT

THE FIRST THANKSGIVING

Written by J.I. Anderson

Illustrated by Gloria McKeown

Troll Associates

10 9 8 7 6 5 4 3 2

Thanksgiving is a wonderful holiday.
It is a time for family, a time for friends.
It is a time for thanks . . . just as
the Pilgrims gave on the first Thanksgiving
over 300 years ago.

Before the
Pilgrims came to America
they lived in England.
But they were not very happy there.

The Pilgrims wanted their religious freedom.

King James had ordered everyone to worship in the Church of England. Those who did not obey him were punished.

JAMES I.

Charter

    With the King's
permission, the Pilgrims
left England to seek their religious freedom.
    They were given a charter to settle in Virginia,
where Captain John Smith had founded the Jamestown colony in 1607.

Two ships set sail. But one leaked very badly and had to turn back. Finally, on September 6, 1620, the *Mayflower* left Plymouth harbor in England and sailed west. Christopher Jones was the captain.

The *Mayflower* carried 102 passengers.
Not all were going to America to seek religious
freedom. Some, like John Alden, were workers
and craftsmen. Others were looking
for a chance to own land, and to
better their lives.

Captain Miles Standish was there
to protect them. The Pilgrims knew
they would be facing danger in the
New World.

The voyage was
not pleasant. The
Mayflower was a small ship.
It was only 90 feet long, and
25 feet wide . . . at most.
Below the deck,
the 102 passengers—men,
women and children—were all
crowded into cramped living
quarters.

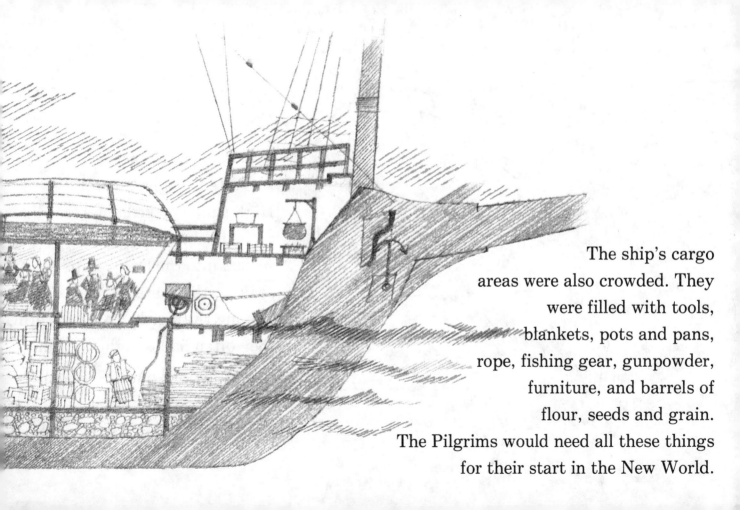

The ship's cargo areas were also crowded. They were filled with tools, blankets, pots and pans, rope, fishing gear, gunpowder, furniture, and barrels of flour, seeds and grain. The Pilgrims would need all these things for their start in the New World.

The voyage across
was often rough and stormy.
High winds rocked and tossed
the ship about. Icy water
seeped into the leaky ship,
soaking the passengers and
making them sick. To keep warm,
they often had to light fires in
cooking pots and huddle together.

There were no beds to sleep on,
no extra water for bathing
or for washing clothes. There
were few hot meals.
Week after week, they
ate cold biscuits, salted
or dried beef, oatmeal
with molasses,
and sometimes—
cheese.

But sometimes on warm sunny days,
when the sea was calm, the passengers
were allowed on deck.
And, while Captain Standish
trained his men,
the children played.

Would it ever end?

After spending over 60 days at sea, many wondered if they would ever see land again.

Then, on the 66th day,
a sailor spotted something far off
in the distance.

"Land ho!" he called . . .
and everyone raced up on deck
to catch a glimpse of
their new home.

On November 11, 1620,
the *Mayflower* dropped its
anchor off the tip of Cape Cod.
Storms had blown
the ship off course. The
Pilgrims were far north
of Virginia. Still,
everyone was happy
and eager to go ashore.

But, before they left the *Mayflower*,
the Pilgrim leaders knew that they needed
a set of laws to govern their life
in the New World. So they
drew up the Mayflower Compact.

The Mayflower Compact was an agreement signed by every man on the ship. They all promised to obey the new laws, and they elected John Carver their first governor.

Then, before anyone could go ashore, Governor Carver sent Captain Standish and several other men to explore the coast to find a good place for a settlement.

The group went ashore and explored
the sandy beaches. They discovered good
water for drinking, small evergreen trees,
and buried Indian corn.

But they sailed still further, until they reached the bay at Plymouth. It had taken nearly a month to find the right place for their settlement. Plymouth seemed safe. It had good land, and a good harbor. It also had a high hill where a fort could be built for protection.

In December the Pilgrims went ashore.
This would be their home!

Now there was work to be done. It was winter and they
wanted to build their houses quickly. They would live
on the *Mayflower* until their houses were ready.

The first building to be built
was the Common House. It was
20 feet long and 20 feet wide, and
it was going to be a prayer and
meeting house. But when the snows
came, the Pilgrims huddled inside
the Common House just to keep warm.
Before long it would be used as
a hospital.

The first winter in Plymouth was hard. The Pilgrims had very little food. Sickness and disease spread quickly among them. By the time winter was over, half were dead. Many remained sick and weak, and all wondered what was ahead in this strange, new land.

Then suddenly, winter
turned to spring. By March,
the sixth house
had been built. The
earth turned green,
the sun was warm,
and flowers seemed
ready to bloom.
There was a feeling of
new life as the Pilgrims
began planting their crops.

One spring day something strange happened.
An Indian walked into the village.
At first, the Pilgrims were frightened.
But the Indian raised his hand
in friendship and said in English,
"Welcome. I am Samoset."
Later, he told the Pilgrims
many things about the land.
He told them how a tribe had once lived
where the Pilgrims were now living.
He also promised to return the
next day with Indian braves who would
trade with them.

Samoset belonged to the Wampanoag tribe. Eventually, Samoset brought his leader, Chief Massasoit, to meet the Pilgrims.

Chief Massasoit and Governor Carver signed a treaty. They agreed to live in peace, share the land, and to help each other.

One of the most interesting Indians Samoset
ever brought to Plymouth was his friend Squanto.
Squanto spoke even better English than Samoset.

Squanto had once lived in England,
having been taken there by boat.

But Squanto was now back in the land
of his birth and was willing
to help the Pilgrims.

Squanto taught the Pilgrims many things. He showed them how to plant corn by using a dead fish for fertilizer. Corn was not grown in England, and it was still a strange, new plant to the Pilgrims.

Squanto showed them how to grind corn to make flour, how to bake with it, and even how to make it pop!

Squanto also showed the Pilgrims how to hunt with a bow and arrow. He showed them berries and nuts in the forest that were safe to eat.

He taught them where to dig for clams, where to catch lobster . . . and where to fish for cod, trout, and eels.

Squanto came to live with the Pilgrims
at Plymouth. That spring, when Captain Jones
sailed back to England on the *Mayflower*,
he wondered what their fate would be.
Fortunately, with Squanto's help,
they would be able to
survive in the
New World.

All spring and all summer, the Pilgrims worked hard in the fields.

In the autumn of 1621, they harvested their first crops. It was a good harvest!

Now there would be plenty of food to help them survive the coming winter.

In October, William Bradford, the new governor, called everyone together. "God has been good to us," he said. "Let us give thanks!"

Everyone began to prepare for a big feast
of thanksgiving. The women worked for days,
baking and cooking. The men went into the
forest to hunt wild turkeys. And the boys
fished for trout in cool, clear streams.

Everyone had a job to do. Young children dug for clams on the beach. Others worked in the kitchen. And still others picked berries and nuts, or gathered firewood.

The Pilgrims did not forget to invite their friends the Indians. Squanto led Chief Massasoit, Samoset, and 90 Wampanoag braves to Plymouth. The Indians brought five deer to add to the feast.

And what a great thanksgiving feast it was!
The Pilgrims wore their best clothes. All
kinds of tasty foods were set on the
long tables.
There was corn bread, cranberries, turkey,
pumpkin, clams, eels, deer, squash
and fish . . . some of the foods that
the Pilgrims had found
in America.

The first Thanksgiving celebration lasted
for three days. There was much fun and laughter.
There were contests and games,
dances and races.

The Pilgrims did not forget to give thanks on that first Thanksgiving. They thanked God for all that was given to them . . . a good harvest, good friends, and a good life in America.